EDGE
BOOKS

MINI-BEAST WARS

SCORPION vs CENTIPEDE

BY KIMBERLY FELTES TAYLOR

DUEL TO THE DEATH

raintree
a Capstone company — publishers for children

Raintree is an imprint of Capstone Global Library Limited, a company incorporated in England and Wales having its registered office at 264 Banbury Road, Oxford, OX2 7DY – Registered company number: 6695582

www.raintree.co.uk
myorders@raintree.co.uk

Printed and bound in China.

ISBN 978 1 4747 1086 2 (hardback)
21 20 19 18 17 16
10 9 8 7 6 5 4 3 2 1

ISBN 978 1 4747 1090 9 (paperback)
21 20 19 18 17 16
10 9 8 7 6 5 4 3 2 1

British Library Cataloguing in Publication Data
A full catalogue record for this book is available from the British Library.

Editorial Credits
Nate LeBoutillier, editor; Russell Griesmer, designer; Katy LaVigne, production specialist

The publisher would like to thank Christiane Weirauch, Professor of Entomology at University of California, Riverside for her help creating this book.

Photo Credits
Alamy: PhotoStock-Israel, 25; Corbis: RooM the Agency/DeepDesertPhoto (RF), 23; Corel, 19 (bottom); Dreamstime: Daniel Mccauley Iv, 29; Getty Images: Digital Vision, 7 (bottom), 15 (bottom), 17 (bottom); Nature Picture Library: Barry Mansell, 27; Science Source: Tom McHugh, 19 (top); Shutterstock: Aleksey Stemmer, Cover, 4, 11 (top), 21, Audrey Snider-Bell, 9 (top), 13 (left), c photospirit, 7, (top), IrinaK, 15 (top), Kittikorn Phongok, 13 (right), RPan Xunbin, 17 (top); Visuals Unlimited/Gerold & Cynthia Merker, Cover, 5, 11 (bottom), 20; Wikimedia: Canley, 9 (bottom)

Design Elements
Capstone and Shutterstock:

Every effort has been made to contact copyright holders of material reproduced in this book. Any omissions will be rectified in subsequent printings if notice is given to the publisher.

All the Internet addresses (URLs) given in this book were valid at the time of going to press. However, due to the dynamic nature of the Internet, some addresses may have changed, or sites may have changed or ceased to exist since publication. While the author and publisher regret any inconvenience this may cause readers, no responsibility for any such changes can be accepted by either the author or the publisher.

CONTENTS

WELCOME TO MINI-BEAST WARS!

Mini-beasts can be ferocious! Some of them have claws and stingers. Others have mouths as sharp as razors. Some even have fangs. They use these weapons to hunt down – and kill – other bugs. Sometimes, they easily crush their **prey**. Other times, they must fight head to head. The fight can end with either mini-beast as the winner.

prey animal hunted by another animal for food

nocturnal active at night and resting during the day

arthropod animal with a hard outer shell and many legs with joints

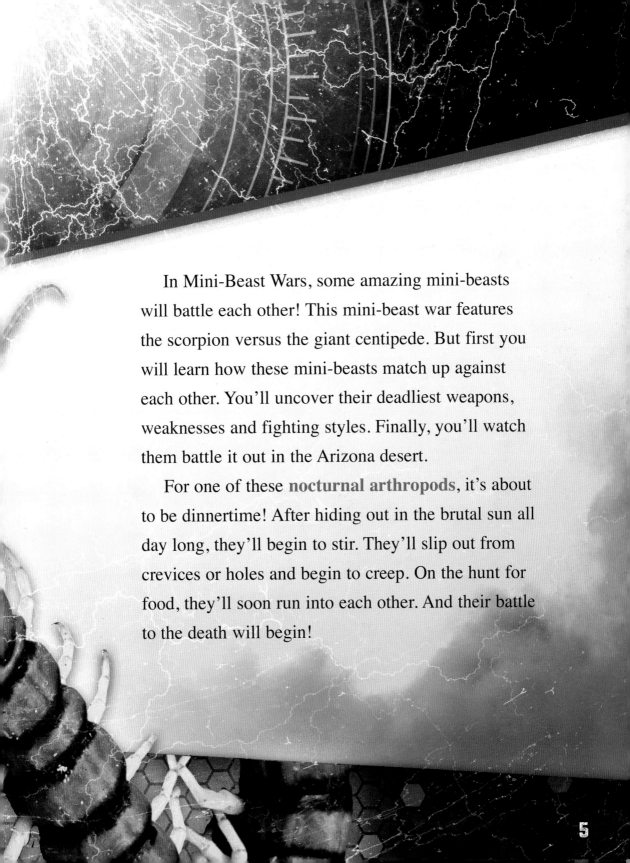

In Mini-Beast Wars, some amazing mini-beasts will battle each other! This mini-beast war features the scorpion versus the giant centipede. But first you will learn how these mini-beasts match up against each other. You'll uncover their deadliest weapons, weaknesses and fighting styles. Finally, you'll watch them battle it out in the Arizona desert.

For one of these **nocturnal arthropods**, it's about to be dinnertime! After hiding out in the brutal sun all day long, they'll begin to stir. They'll slip out from crevices or holes and begin to creep. On the hunt for food, they'll soon run into each other. And their battle to the death will begin!

THE COMBATANTS

The bark scorpion and the giant centipede are both found in northern Mexico and the southwestern part of the United States. But they are most commonly spotted in the Arizona desert. These two creatures prey on a wide variety of mini-beasts, including each other. When they meet up, they almost always fight – often to the death!

The battle between these two well-matched arthropods can be lengthy. One reason for the long death matches is that both mini-beasts have **exoskeletons**, or outside skeletons. Humans have endoskeletons, or skeletons inside their bodies. These mini-beasts' hard outer skeletons help protect them like armour during battle.

FIERCE FACT

THERE ARE MORE THAN 1,500 SPECIES OF SCORPION AND MORE THAN 3,000 SPECIES OF CENTIPEDES.

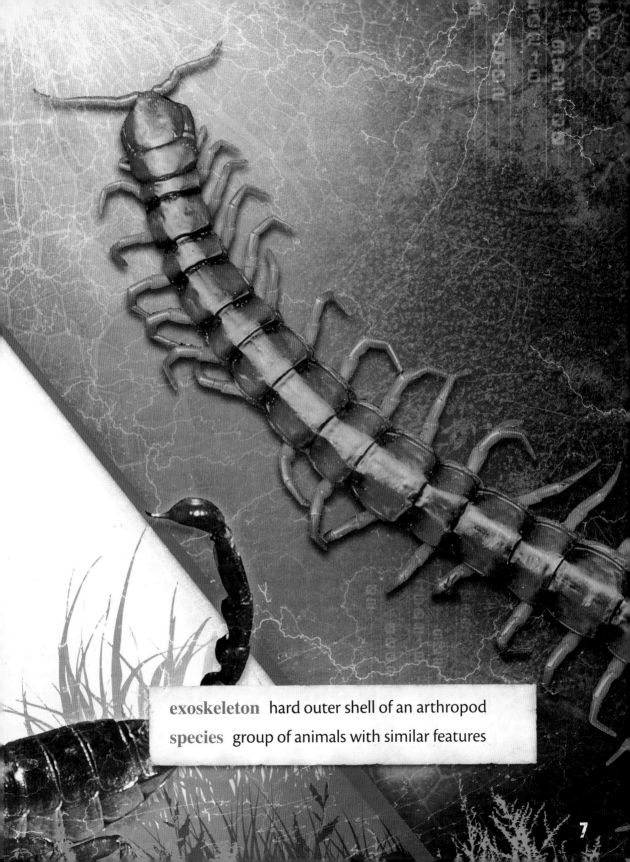

exoskeleton hard outer shell of an arthropod

species group of animals with similar features

SIZE

The bark scorpion grows up to 7.6 centimetres
(3 inches) long. That might sound tiny. But the bark
scorpion would probably stretch across the full width
of your palm. (Now imagine this deadly creature
scurrying up your arm and ready to sting. It doesn't
sound so tiny now, does it?) Compared to other
mini-beasts, the bark scorpion is big. Most species of
termites, beetles, spiders and many other mini-beasts
do not even grow to be 2.5 cm (1 in) long.

The giant centipede is called a "giant" for good
reason. It grows up to 20 cm (8 in) long. That's
huge in the world of mini-beasts! With extra length
comes extra weight. So the giant centipede has more
power than smaller mini-beasts. In a giant centipede's
battle with a bark scorpion, the centipede has the
size advantage.

But don't count the scorpion out. All that extra
centipede length just means one thing to the fearless
scorpion – more to grab onto with its pincers!

RATING 1.5

SCORPION:
tiny trooper

RATING 3.5

CENTIPEDE:
super squiggly

FIERCE FACT

THE LARGEST SCORPION IS THE EMPEROR SCORPION.
IT GROWS UP TO 20 CM (8 IN) LONG AND LIVES IN WESTERN
AFRICA. THE AMAZONIAN CENTIPEDE, THE LARGEST
CENTIPEDE, GROWS UP TO 35 CM (14 IN) IN LENGTH
AND IS FOUND IN SOUTH AMERICA.

SPEED AND AGILITY

The bark scorpion is speedy when it wants to be. Its legs are jointed. So it can quickly move forward – or even leap – to attack.

The bark scorpion's legs end in claws. These claws help it move nimbly over sand, rocks or objects in its path. No terrain is too tough for this deadly creature.

The giant centipede is also a fast mover. Most have 21 to 23 pairs of legs, giving them **agility**. Each pair of legs works together, and the pairs move in waves. In this way, centipedes can appear to slither like a snake.

Unlike the scorpion, the centipede cannot move its entire body to the right or the left in just one or two steps. But it does move sideways more often than the scorpion. To go sideways, the centipede curves its head left or right to set a new direction. Then the body follows.

agility ability to move quickly and easily

RATING
3

SCORPION:
fast forward

RATING
3.5

CENTIPEDE:
multi-mover

FIERCE FACT

HOUSE CENTIPEDES ARE VERY FAST BUT GROW TO JUST 3.8 CM (1.5 IN) LONG. THEY LIVE IN BASEMENTS, BATHROOMS AND WARDROBES. THEY EAT OTHER INSECTS, SUCH AS BE BUGS AND TERMITES, THAT YOU REALLY DON'T WANT LIVING IN YOUR HOUSE.

WEAPONS

The bark scorpion's first deadly weapons are **pincers**. The pincers are located on either side of its head. The scorpion uses its pincers to grab and crush smaller prey. With larger prey, the scorpion uses its pincers to hold. This keeps prey from running away or fighting back.

The scorpion has a second deadly weapon – a stinger. The stinger is located at the end of the scorpion's tail. It plunges the stinger into prey and releases venom, **paralysing** the prey. Then the scorpion starts to eat the prey alive.

The giant centipede uses its fangs as a weapon. The fangs look like its first pair of legs. But they are not legs. After the centipede bites into prey, it releases venom through its fangs. The venom numbs the prey and poisons the prey's **nervous system**. The prey stops moving and dies.

The giant centipede's many legs are another weapon. It uses its legs to grab and hold, like the scorpion uses its **pincers**.

FIERCE FACT

SCORPION VENOM CAN BE DEADLY TO HUMANS – BUT IT IS ALSO PROVING TO BE HELPFUL. THE VENOM FROM SOME SCORPIONS CAN BE USED AS "TUMOUR PAINT". THE VENOM IS USED TO LOCATE CANCER CELLS IN A HUMAN. THEN A SURGEON OPERATES AND REMOVES THE CANCER CELLS.

RATING 4

SCORPION:
super stinger

RATING 4

CENTIPEDE:
lightning legged

pincer   claw used to hold prey

paralyse   cause a loss of ability to control the muscles

nervous system   brain, spinal cord and nerves; the nervous system controls all body functions

DEFENCES

The bark scorpion's main defence is its yellow-brown colour. This creature is not easy to see when on rock, sand, dirt and – of course – tree bark.

What happens if a **predator** spots the bark scorpion? The scorpion adopts a threatening pose. It spreads its pincers wide. It raises its stinger high into the air. It hopes to scare off the predator.

The giant centipede uses colour as a defence too. But not to hide. Rather, its red and black body and yellow legs are meant to look threatening.

Furthermore, the colouring makes the head and tail look alike. So predators don't know which end to attack. If they attack the tail, the centipede can quickly curl its head around and dig its fangs into the predator.

The giant centipede can also easily curl up to avoid attack. The centipede is very **flexible** because of its many segments. This flexibility gives the giant centipede the advantage in self-defence.

predator animal that hunts other animals for food
flexible able to bend

FIERCE FACT

SOME SPECIES OF CENTIPEDE CAN SHED SOME OF THEIR LEGS WHEN ATTACKED. THE LEGS KEEP WRIGGLING. THE PREDATOR GOES AFTER THE LEGS. THE CENTIPEDE DARTS AWAY.

RATING 3.5

CENTIPEDE:
flexi-fighter

RATING 2.5

SCORPION:
big time
blender

WEAKNESSES

The bark scorpion can have up to six pairs of eyes. But it has poor vision. It can only tell if it is dark or light.

To "see", the bark scorpion relies on its sense of touch. Scorpions have sensors called **sensilla**. The sensilla is located mostly on the legs and body. The sensilla help scorpions feel the shaking of the ground when something moves. This shaking lets the scorpion know where things are and if they are coming or going.

The giant centipede also has poor vision. Like the bark scorpion, its eyes can only tell light from dark. So it relies mostly on its antennae to feel and smell prey and predators. The **antennae** are long, agile, and in constant motion.

Unlike the bark scorpion, the giant centipede does not have any sensors. It only has its antennae. So the giant centipede is the slight loser when it comes to weaknesses.

antennae feelers on the head of an insect or arthropod used to sense movement

sensilla simple sense organ consisting of one or a few cells at the end of a sensory nerve fibre

RATING 1

CENTIPEDE:
image impaired

FIERCE FACT

SOME SPECIES OF CENTIPEDES DO NOT HAVE ANY EYES!

RATING 1.5

SCORPION:
lousy lookers

ATTACK STYLE

The bark scorpion hunts alone. First, it finds a place to sit and wait for prey. If prey moves towards the scorpion, it stays very still. The scorpion wants prey to come as close as possible. When the prey is close enough, the scorpion lunges. It grabs onto the prey with its pincers. If needed, it uses its stinger. Then the scorpion starts to eat.

The giant centipede is also a lone hunter. But unlike the scorpion, it doesn't wait around for prey. It seeks it out. Once it detects prey, the centipede moves quickly towards it. The centipede grabs onto the prey with its fangs. It releases its venom. It might curl its body around the prey to keep it still until the venom kicks in. Even so, the scorpion's surprise-attack method gives it a slight advantage.

FIERCE FACT

SCORPIONS ARE CANNIBALS. THEY WILL EAT OTHER SCORPIONS – EVEN THEIR OWN FAMILY MEMBERS!

RATING

3.5

CENTIPEDE:
heroic hunter

RATING

3

SCORPION:
surprise stalker

GET READY TO RUMBLE!

This mini-beast battle will definitely be fierce. In one corner is the relentless chaser – the giant centipede. In the other corner is the surprise attacker – the bark scorpion. Both mini-beasts are fearless warriors. And both are determined to kill and eat each other.

BEFORE THE BATTLE BEGINS . . .

This battle is made-up, just like your favourite film. But the battle could happen in real life. These two types of mini-beasts really do hunt each other. They really do fight. And every time, one of the mini-beasts really does win.

Now, for our battle. Who will win? And who will end up as dinner?

HUNT TO THE DEATH!

The sun has almost set in the Arizona desert. Ironwood trees and cacti cast long shadows in the last of the dim light. The bark scorpion – ready to eat – crawls out of a crevice in a rock wall. It scurries down the wall. It starts to wander along a dusty path. The path is lined with pebbles and short shrub. It has no trouble hopping around, or even over, these obstacles.

Suddenly, the scorpion stops. Its sensors have picked up movement. It backs up and hides just behind a rock. There it waits.

Just a few rocks to the right, a giant centipede is slowly wriggling along another path. It has no idea that it is heading towards the scorpion.

FIERCE FACT

PREGNANT FEMALE SCORPIONS ARE THE FIERCEST. THE EXTRA WEIGHT THEY CARRY WITH THE PREGNANCY MAKES IT DIFFICULT FOR THEM TO SCURRY AWAY FROM PREDATORS. SO THEY ARE QUICK TO USE THEIR STINGERS.

FIRST STRIKE

The scorpion waits, keeping very still. The centipede comes into the scorpion's sight. The centipede keeps moving along its path, still unaware of the scorpion. At just the right moment, the scorpion lunges but misses.

The centipede, using its antenna to quickly locate the scorpion, veers towards the scorpion, ready for a fight. The scorpion takes an offensive pose – pincers spread, stinger raised. But the centipede doesn't pause. It zooms towards the scorpion.

The scorpion hops left and right to dodge the centipede. Recognizing the perfect moment, the scorpion springs towards the centipede again – this time, with success! It grabs onto the centipede's head with its pincers. The centipede can't possibly dig its fangs into the scorpion under this grip.

But the centipede isn't ready to give up. It coils around the scorpion defensively, ready to squeeze the scorpion with its entire body. Can the scorpion out-wrestle the centipede?

FIERCE FACT

THE GIANT AMAZONIAN CENTIPEDE IS SO FIERCE AND POWERFUL THAT IT CAN CATCH BATS IN MID-FLIGHT.

CHARGE!

The scorpion knows it is in a bad position. It flings the centipede away before the centipede can wrap its body around him. The centipede crashes against a rock and is briefly stunned. The scorpion takes advantage of this moment and charges at the centipede's head again.

But the scorpion has mistaken the centipede's tail for its head. The scorpion lunges at the wrong end. This mistake gives the centipede time to recover. It quickly curls its head towards the scorpion, ready to dig its fangs into the scorpion.

The scorpion senses the error, though. It quickly changes its course and scurries up the rock wall. Then, it circles back around and hovers over the centipede. The scorpion lunges again – this time, at the centipede's mid-section. It catches the centipede and digs in with its pincers.

The centipede once again curls its head around towards the scorpion. The centipede wants to dig its fangs into the scorpion and release its venom.

MOST SPECIES OF
CENTIPEDE ARE HARMLESS
TO HUMANS. BUT THE
GIANT CENTIPEDE WILL
BITE HUMANS. THE BITE
CAN BE PAINFUL, THOUGH
NOT DEADLY.

A FINAL STING

The centipede's fangs come closer and closer to the scorpion. But the scorpion does not let go. Instead, once again, it waits. When the centipede's head – and fangs – are very close, the scorpion whips its tail around. It plunges its stinger into the centipede's head. The scorpion's venom quickly takes effect. The centipede is paralysed and lies motionless. It's a victory for the scorpion!

Now that the scorpion has captured its dinner, it must prepare the meal. It tears the centipede into pieces. It spits digestive juices on each piece. The digestive juices break down the centipede pieces into mush. After the digestive juices have done their job, the scorpion begins to suck up the mush. A slow eater, the scorpion enjoys its meal for hours.

FIERCE FACT

IN GREEK MYTHOLOGY, A GIANT SCORPION CALLED SCORPIO KILLED THE GREAT HUNTER ORION. WHEN THE GODS PUT THEM IN THE SKY AS CONSTELLATIONS, OR GROUPS OF STARS, THEY PUT THEM FAR APART. THIS KEPT SCORPIO AND ORION FROM FIGHTING.

GLOSSARY

agility ability to move quickly and easily

antennae feelers on the head of an insect or arthropod used to sense movement

arthropod animal with a hard outer shell and many legs with joints

exoskeleton hard outer shell of an arthropod

flexible able to bend

nervous system brain, spinal cord and nerves; the nervous system controls all body functions

nocturnal active at night and resting during the day

paralyse to cause a loss of ability to control the muscles

pincer claw used to hold prey

predator animal that hunts other animals for food

prey animal hunted by another animal for food

sensilla simple sense organ consisting of one or a few cells at the end of a sensory nerve fibre

species group of animals with similar features

READ MORE

Amazing Animal Predators (Animal Superpowers), John Townsend (Raintree, 2013)

Crazy Creepy Crawlies (Extreme Animals), Isabel Thomas (Raintree, 2013)

The Life Cycle of Insects (Life Cycles), Susan Heinrichs Gray (Raintree, 2012)

WEBSITES

www.britannica.com/animal/scorpion
Find out more about the many species of scorpion, their features and their behaviours.

www.britannica.com/animal/centipede
Find out more about the many species of centipede, their features and their behaviours.

INDEX